Adventures on Earth

Gerald Braude

ISBN: 978-93-6354-495-6

First Edition: 2026
Rs. 200/-

Cyberwit.net
HIG 45 Kaushambi Kunj, Kalindipuram
Allahabad - 211011 (U.P.) India
http://www.cyberwit.net
Tel: +(91) 9415091004
E-mail: info@cyberwit.net

Printed at Repro.

For Karen

Contents

Communications

Carrier Pigeon

You are a beautiful
wounded bird.

When you fly away,
at times I'm certain

you'll never come back.
But you always do.

I can only promise
you this.

I will never clip
your wings.

Robin's Nest

Apple and pear trees stand over a faraway,
vacant field. Entangled deep into the bunch
grass and broken branches is a fractured
ethernet cable.

Faraway stands a greenhouse with a robin's
nest perched atop a rafter.
"I don't know how it got there,
but it's got to go," she says.

Under her orders, he carries the ladder
from the storage shed into the greenhouse.
As he climbs to the top of the ladder, she explains
she doesn't want them pecking at her plants.

He reaches as high as he can and brushes
the dried fibers of grass and small twigs
onto the floor, his hands freckled
with smudges of dirt.

"Now for the mysterious problem of all,"
she says. As they stroll together to the ditch
running alongside the road, they discuss
plans for attending her friend's party.

She stops and stands akimbo atop
a red patch of clay and barks
that the county maintenance tractor
had cut her internet cable.

"My damn ex-boyfriend was so poor, he installed
the cable himself and ran it along the ditch leading
to this road." She adds not even her previous
guys or ex-husband were this cheap.

When he asks her why she has spent all day
digging up brush in search for the cable,
she says, "So that I can splice
it back together or something like that."

So, with a Weed Wacker, she clears
the brush lying over the ditch leading
to the road, while he digs up the dirt
with his hands.

"The cable's got to be here," they keep
saying to each other, amidst the flying
bunches of grass, brambles, dirt and dust,
but it turns out not to be there.

After the sun falls beneath the treetops,
she says she's heading inside to clean up
for the party, but knowing his tenacity,
she is sure he'll find that cable.

And so as his knees lead him
toward the road, he digs and digs,
sweat pouring onto the clumps
of dirt on his hands and forearms.

He stops at where the two ditches intersect.
On the other side of the road, a sprinkler hose hangs
from a chain linked fence. He says to his cramped
knees, "I can't help her with this anymore."

Spirit of Marriage

I learned to be faithful,
and she was there.

I learned unconditional love,
and she was there.

I learned how to be a father,
and she was there.

I learned to keep my body pure,
and she was there.

I learned to fuel my passions,
and she was there.

I learned to love the mountains,
and she was there.

I learned to count my blessings every day,
and she was there.

Life does not get any better
than this.

The Courting Game

The sun beamed
down on me. She
was in the shadows.

I knew her
as someone who
swung for the fences.

The count was
three balls,
two strikes.

I lobbed to her
a nice, smooth,
easy one.

A waist-high toss
that could make us
both a winner.

Her eyes, green
as the infield, stared
at the passing ball.

The umpire raised,
then pumped his arm,
and bellowed, "Steeerike three."

Harmony

I could hear
but not see
Sky Mountain River.

I strolled alongside bushes
of berries, my thoughts caught
up in sporadic streets of shit.

A bear appeared
at the bend beside
the row of bushes.

He perked up and showed
me the biggest ears
I've ever seen on a bear.

I stopped in my tracks
and slowly backpedaled
and backpedaled some more.

He was out of my sight
until he gingerly climbed
up a slope to my right.

He crawled into a fortress
of trees and was
out of my sight.

I stopped and stumbled
among some rock edges.
My heart pounded.
How was I going to get
out of this mess?

I pulled out my headlamp
from my backpack. The beam
would keep him away.

I hit the "on" button.
My heart sank. The batteries
were dead.

Brain fog consumed me. I pulled
out my mp3 player. Finally, I had
use for the external speaker.

Soothing classical music
came to mind. My shaking
fingers pushed the icons.

I settled on Debussy's
Orchestration of Satie's
Gymnopedie Number One.

I steadily tiptoed alongside
the flow of the oboes' melody atop
of the cellos' sustained bass lines.

"It's okay, bear" I said in pleading
tones." I mean no harm.
I'm harmless."

When I got to the first flowing notes
from the flutes, the bear burst out
from the bushes.

He growled, ‘Will you knock
that shit off.” He then led me
by the paw to the river’s edge.

Sparkling water skipped freely
down the rock ledges
into a gently flowing pool of aqua.

The real sound of oboes flowing
atop of grounded cellos. The
bear pointed at the sight.

“I don’t know what in the world you
people are doing down there,” he said.
“But up here, everything makes sense.”

It Feels So Good

The little log cabin resort experiences
sundown and quiet time.

Just the flow from the river
reverberates through the forested canyon.

Until.

“How come you didn’t fill my water bottle?”
“I did.”
“But it’s empty.”
“That’s because you drank it all.”
“I did not.”

“Where’s my watch?”
“What makes you think I know where it is?”
“Because it’s your job to make sure I know what time it is?”
“Well, use mine then.”
“You know I can’t do that. It’s too slow.”

A knock on the door.
It creaks open.

“Will you two please stop bickering.”
“What are you talking about? We never bicker.”
“That’s right.”
“How dare you make this accusation.”
“That’s right. We never, ever bicker.”

Scenic View

The backcountry trail took me
from towering firs and cedars
to a highway rest area
that always felt just right.

Sticking to my creature of habit
instincts, I sat cross-legged
with my back against the outside
wall to the men's restroom.

The parking lot clearing afforded
an unobstructed view of the glacier-peaked
mountain just below a puffy hanging cloud.
I breathed in deeply and took it all in.

But then came that darn janitor pushing
his cart of cleaning gear. As he was
about to pass me, we greeted each
othcr by namc. Hc stoppcd.

I swallowed hard. He sidestepped
and directly towered over me.
I asked him to move, but he kept yelling,
"Rigged, rigged, rigged."

I closed my eyelids nearly all the way,
imagining the mountain I could
not see. It quivered as his voice
drowned out the highway traffic.

"I've never seen so many dead
people vote in my life," he rattled.
I mentioned the protest; steam popped
out from the fumarole.

"Yeah right; earmuff man and thin-hair
man stepping out from behind police
lines and leading the charge
to the Speaker's Lobby."

I was atop of the floating cloud
for a bird's eye view of the erupting gas,
ash, and rocks as I mentioned the stolen
laptop from the senator's office.

"He said that because he's a liberal. Only liberals
like Pelosi block Jordan and Banks from the committee
and use pseudo conservatives. "Even my wife
wouldn't do that, and she's a liberal, but we get along fine."

I could see lava spewing from the top
as he said, "But I will survive all this shit
because I always get my twelve dollars an hour,
and I know how to shoot and skin a deer."

I swear I saw the lava chase the deer
down the slopes as he said, "So what
do you think of them apples?" I widened
my eyes: "That was some scenic view."

Fighting for Airspace

"We'll be right back with more
from your Sports Mama after a word
from our sponsors, so don't even think
of touching that dial."

Her rounded chin dangles
inches away from the mic.
The door cracks open,
barely enough for her to hear,

"Ratings are dropping."
She says,
"Got it boss, you be
the third call."

She leans forward,
wiggling her fanny
against both armrests.
After two calls, game on.

"Yeah, um, thanks for taking
my call, um."

"Just get to the point,
Will ya?"

"Well, um, Lakers all the way,
man."

"No, you're not a man.
No man ever roots for purple
and yellow. Those are faggot
colors, you idiot. There's only one
man's team out there:
the Celtics.

"Yeah, um, green agenda.
Save mother earth, man."

"Not that kind of green,
you faggot. I'm talking dollar
green and white. Made for man.
That's why your Sports Mama makes
the Celtics the all-time champs and this
country great, and only a wimp like you would
mess with me, so don't ever think of calling me again."

Indelible

The world swirls
senselessly at me.

It's enough to scare
anyone to pieces.

But I hold the life
together metaphor.

I love
my pen.

Double I's

I'm so tired of this,
I'm seeing double
as I jot
into my log:

I much prefer staying
alone

than amidst
a bunch
of
Intoxicated Idiots.

Courtesy

"So, what would you
like to talk about next?"

"Nothing."

"Well then, since I see
I'm boring
the shit out of you,
I'll let you go
talk to somebody else."

"Okay. Thank you."

Country Living

You don't truly know

your county until
you've been living

on a carved out
gravel road

with potholes.

Little Log Cabin in the Lane

Please don't envy
my lifestyle values.
To do so
diminishes yours.

Control

Operant Conditioning

Your attention, please.
This is a message
from the emergency
broadcasting system.

This is not a test.
We repeat. This is not
a test. The emergency
has been lifted. That's right.
Life is back to normal!

And we have you to thank
for that. We thank you for trusting
and following our orders:

Pulling your children out of school.
Locking yourself up in your cells.
Putting on masks.

Most important, you faithfully took
the vaccines, and because you
trusted us enough to do as told,
our lives can go back to normal.

"These sacks are heavy."
"Yep."
"Do you think they'll catch up to us?"
"*Qué va!* We're cruising
at the speed of science."

The Needle

Which
do you
fear more?

Mankind
or
nature?

Spinning Out of Control

The atomic bomb set the1947 Doomsday Clock
to seven minutes to midnight.

Not to be undone, the nuclear bomb set
the1949 Doomsday Clock to four minutes to midnight.

The 2007 climate change moved the hands
even closer to midnight.

Sometimes that clock gives us a few more minutes
to work with. The 2009 Arctic clock allowed five
years before it would run out of ice.

The 1989 rising sea levels clock allowed
eleven years before nations would be wiped
off the face of the Earth.

The 1995 rising sea levels clock allowed
a quarter century until most of the beaches
on the East Coast of the United States would be gone.

Are the hands now straying too far from midnight?
Okay, how about the 2014 clock saying we have
only five hundred days before we hit climate chaos.

Is that still not close enough?
Okay, how about the squawk
all our ham radios just got:

We're all gonna die
yesterday, or was
it the day before?

Fact Finding Mission

I end my daily
log entries as follows:

How can a species
so smart be so stupid?

Bluff River Valley

Haze and gossip hover
over the table.
It is his turn
to deal.

On the TV,
a caveman claws
at the window.
Dr. Smith screams.

The cards dart
out of his hands
to the circle
of bearded men.

The countdown
from seven begins.
Yellow scraggly letters stand
out from the Milky Way.

He draws one card,
then studies
his pair
of jacks.

The Jupiter II shrinks in size,
then snaps into scraggly letters:
"Lost
in
Space"

He whistles along
with the ascending
frantic lines
from the brass section.

Next to the TV, the door creaks
open a bit. A long pavement colored
beard, then a pair of rounded spectacles
appear through the crack.

In rhythm with the rain pellets
against the cemented porch,
he says,
"The aliens are here. The aliens are here."

The dealer aims
an even stare at him.
"Not right now,
Sam."

"Really, they just let
'em cross the river.
A flood of them
are coming at us."

He shoves a wad of bills
to the center of the table.
"I'm going to raise you
on two kings."

The two black beards with streaks
of gray along each side throw
down their cards
and bolt out the door.

The final one pulls at the tip
of his gray beard, lays down
his pair of queens, and grunts
on his way out the door.

The dealer lowers
his elbows
and embraces
the pile of money.

A smile hidden beneath
his dark moustache, he
contemplatively rubs
his bare chin.

He steps outside to the shrinking
clouds scurrying along the sky's
glass ceiling while the wind lashes
at the scattered rabbitbrush.

A sign posted in front
of the general store reads,
"State of Emergency.
No Background checks."

All the patrons are ahead of him
in line. They point their rifles
to the window. A shiny cloud shaped
like a short screw shoots a bronzed-yellow bolt.

The sky echoes a slow squeak.
When it sounds more like a rusty jar

unscrewing, they bolt past the cashier
and stumble out the door.

He strolls out the store
with his slabs of wood,
a paper bag of bolts, a can
of paint, and his sharpened saw.

He passes the elongated blasts of rifles
and staccato snaps of pistols from Gun
Club Road, then stops at the driveway
that winds up the bluff to his home.

Thumps from his shovel, bangs from his
hammer, swooshes from his can of spray paint
reverberate against white cumulus clouds
rimmed with silver that bang like kettledrums.

Amidst the wisps of smoke from the valley
below, his neighbors stand on the lookout
from their porches, brandishing their guns
and sipping their beers.

Until, as if spotting a mirage
in the wavering desert sand,
they rush to a sign at the edge
of the road.

One pulls at the tip of his beard, and says,
"Well I'll be a son of a …"

One squints, scratches his beard, and says,
"And I'll be damned."

One freezes as if too numb
to say anything at all.

Finally, shaking their heads,
they depart from a sign
that reads in drooping letters,
"I sleep in bed with a gun."

Security Services

How many enemies
does it take
to be a billionaire?

How about a president?
How about a governor?
How about a political prisoner?

Papers Please

They approached with such white complexions
the inhabitants of Red Rock Country
thought for sure they were ghosts.

But if they were from the Great Spirit, why were
they asking for directions and for scouts to guide
them through the surrounding areas?

The ghosts said they came
from a continent beyond
the waters of the rising sun.

Now since they're done with fighting a civil war,
they were destined to make life better for the savages
so long as they behaved themselves.

And so for their own good, the savages were told
their days of running wild to gather grass seeds and hunt
for antelope and deer were forever in the past.

They were to learn on the land reserved for them
the habits of industrious farming and cattle-raising
to attain the permanence of wealth and distinction.

For their own safety and protection,
they were issued
identification tags:

Crosses, crescents, circles, diamonds, squares, triangles,
specifying a particular band, each with the number
of its owner punched upon it.

If one of them strayed too far,
he would have to show his pass,
and it better correspond with the tags worn.

Seven or so generations later, the folks at Red Rock Country
get the ghosts' news from hard-earned TVs, which tells
them they're getting a new set of tags to keep
up with the technocratic era—the digital ID.

With jaws dropped while eyeing the screens,
they learn such tags as vaccine passports
are being issued from not just the ghosts
of this nation but of nineteen other nations.

One turns his gaze from the screen and tells
another, "It's not just us but a planetary takeover."
Sure enough, the screen tells them for the global
good fifteen minute cities will be implemented.

It all sounds too familiar when they learn
this worldwide effort will use license plate
recognition to track and fine drivers
who leave their designated zones.

One slaps a hand on his knee and laughs
to the other, "Before you know it, for their own
good, the rest of the planet won't be allowed
to hunt for antelope or deer, either."

Contemporary Circuitry

I stroll across the bridge
above the white caps
on the river.

I pause to sketch into my notepad
a lichen covered rock blocking
a tree from toppling into the rapids.

A Tesla passes by and stops.
The driver and passenger jump
out, take photos with their iPhones.

They hop back in and skid
a few more yards until reaching
the campground entrance.

The driver rolls down his window
and holds the face of his iPhone
to a sign posted to a tree.

I pause as I reach the sign.
The envelope box and fee
cannister are nowhere in sight.

Sure enough, the sign reads,
"No cash or checks allowed
for camping fees."

I jot into my notebook how shameful
it is one cannot function
on this planet without a digital device.

Deep State of Mind

The plandemic is over.
The backlash is well on its way.
A new health and human services
secretary is calling the shots.

A man takes a window seat
on the 220 for the long haul to DC.
The sun struggles through its morning
rise above the smoldering bay and
academy of armed sailors.

He wipes his forehead, brushing
against the Bluetooth earmuffs
covering his black, bushy hair.
A black N95 covers his nose and mouth.

The sleeves on his trim jacket extend
past his wrists. Holding it chest high,
he does nothing but finger the face
of his iPhone.

Self Employed

I really needed a coffee kick,
but more important, I had to pee.
At last, I spotted my savior
just beyond a Chase bank.

I pulled into the Starbuck's parking lot
and envisioned those perfectly private restrooms
where I've at times rinsed my body after camping
on the street somewhere between road gigs.

I scurried to the front door and pulled it. Damn,
it was locked. I looked up to the sign. "Lobby closed,
please use drive-thru window." I returned
to the wheel, got in line with the rest of the sheep.

Every few minutes or so, I nudged ahead one
car length, until I finally heard through the speaker
box, "Hello, welcome to Starbucks. I'll be
with you in one moment."

And so I waited for that moment to arise. And waited
until … "Hello, welcome to Starbucks; what can
I get started for you?" I told the box I wanted the smallest
coffee you got 'cause that's all I got room for.

When I finally made it to the window,
grabbed my cup, and told the barista
to keep the change, I asked how
the remodeling was going in the lobby.

The barista hesitated,
then told me the lobby
was closed because the shop
was short on help.

I pulled back onto the road,
where on the sidewalk a lady
in rags held the hand of a girl
portraying hunger-deep eyes.

A baby stroller was tilted
toward them.
They stood behind a sign:
"Spare change needed."

What Is the Exchange Rate?

To Stephen Kinzer

One morning, I woke up in the bunker of a United States Embassy
next to a barrel filled with cash. The CIA operatives counted it up:
One million dollars and thank you, Uncle Sam.

One question remained: How to best spend it.

Fortunately, a man whose passport read "scar on right side
of forehead" but carried a greater distinction as Teddy
Roosevelt's grandson slipped into the bunker
under a pseudonym.

In a soft-spoken, confident tone, he gave his orders.

Spend $150,000 to bribe journalists, editors, preachers,
and other opinion leaders to make the prime minister look bad.
Spend $11,000 per week, a nice chunk of change in 1953,
to bribe members of parliament.
Spend $135,000 to bribe a friendly dictator
to take over the country.

Pay demonstrators to converge on parliament to dismiss
the prime minister.
Hire thugs to attack the prime minister's opposition leaders
to make him look bad.

In a trance of disbelief, I even saw him in the bunker offer
$50,000 to two agents to have their street gang connections

shout their allegiance to the prime minister while breaking
windows, beating bystanders, and shooting at mosques.

The agents said the task was too risky to take on.
He cooly smiled down on them and said if they did not
accept his offer, he would kill them. The agents left
the bunker with a briefcase full of $50,000.

Personally, I liked the prime minister for his passionate belief
in nationalism and democracy, but those dreams came to an end
when the mob of demonstrators, police officers, and soldiers
led by Shaban the Brainless stormed his house.

Some pulled doors, windows, and appliances
onto the sidewalk. Others set fires.
That was some sight: People haggling over the prices
of the goods as the flames lit up the night behind them.

But it was not as disgusting as when I got back
to the embassy, where the operators danced
around a narrow room, occasionally whacking
one another on the back.

Diplomats on the embassy staff came down
and looked at them curiously. They asked nothing,
and Roosevelt's grandson told them nothing.

Had I been able to, I would have said to them,
"It never ceases to amaze me how much this world
can be manipulated with money."

Continuum

Historic District

Central Park West
Where all the people rest

Let's go down
To find a real sound

Central Park West
Where Coltrane is the best

Birds fly high
With each note in the sky

He blows the horn
Wherever birds are born

Generational Wealth

A star in the twilight.
Fame, fortune.
You name it,
he had it.

Save that black hole.
He gazed up at it,
peeking at him
through the cathedral ceiling.

"May God grant me a son!"
His mother, next to him
on the pew, placed a finger
onto his lips.

She whispered into his ear,
"No longer
your spirit
will bc dcplctcd."

With vigor none had seen in her before,
she arranged the dance parties. More like ladies
in tightly fit costumes and glittering makeup
parading across the stage.

Before you knew it,
he picked out the wife
to bring him his spirited
brood of children.

After they came
and family immortality
was persevered, he
knocked on his mother's door.

She phoned the family lawyer,
and he drew up a marital
amendment that not even a slave
would accept.

And so the divorce
proceedings began.

Motherhood

He dashed to the front door,
Behind him, fireworks and singsongs
of Auld Lang Syne were loud and clear.

He opened the door.
He gleamed at his wife's heart
shaped face. "Happy New Year
means time to kiss your loved one."

She strolled past him, looking
down at their son.
"I already did."

A decade and a divorce later,
she enters a café, saunters to a table
topped with heart-shaped doilies
and Queen of Hearts playing cards.

Friends wave to her. She places
a hand on her daughter's shoulder
and gleams. "This is my valentine."

A Father's Struggle

How is it
that I can say

the most important
person
in my life

is no longer
a man?

Circles

To this day, I remember
I was getting a little cocky
as a youth soccer coach.

One year, my team
went undefeated.

The next year, near season's
end, my team was undefeated.
So was my opponent.

Off the field, we were
all buddies.

But now, we kicked hard,
we hit hard, we
spit, and we swore.

At thc final whistle, our team
hung our heads in defeat.

All because the referee made a bad call.

But give the poor teen a break.
Players on our town's high school
team had to ref our games.

Nowadays, that girl is
a mother of three daughters.

She paces the sidelines, yelling
out instructions to her youngest
and the rest of her team.

From the other sidelines,
my son does the same
with his son and team.

They were all buddies
turned into rivals.

But this time, my son and his
team raise their arms in victory.

All because the referee made a bad call.

A Long, Long Life

She wrapped her fingers
around her diploma.
But deep in her soul, she
only wanted immortality.

She wasn't getting
any dates
until through family arrangements
she never understood, she found hope.

She never loved her husband.

When they returned to their house
after running her father's store,
she dutifully cooked dinner
for everyone and then always found
the TV guide for that wimp.

She spent her evenings
next to him
on the couch
in front of the TV.

Whenever he wiggled
his neck,
she massaged the back of it
for as long as …

Well, her two daughters often quipped
that's how she got her arthritis.

But the pain got worse.
Soon after she found herself
as a widow,
her daughters died.

Still, she had good reason for hope.
She had a grandson.

She moved from one coast to the other.
With renewed energy
as a hands-on Grandma,
she gave him everything she had.

The most important person
in her life
would grow up to be a big,
strong man.

But within reach of one hundred
years, as she lay flat on her hospital
bed and saw him for the last time, she shook
her fist at him, as they argued about his femineity.

Lifecycle

I'm in town for my father's
one-hundredth birthday.

In the other room, my brother
and I share problems

we have with our
grown-up kids.

When visiting our father
a half century ago,

we shared
the problems we had with him.

As grownups, our kids have
never met.

If they did, what would they
talk about?

Elon

I don't know
what I did wrong,
but I really blew
it.

Before turning
off the bed lamp,
I clicked onto my
emails.

An interview popped
up about deadnaming
and the woke mind
virus.

But why should
I allow
his problems to be my
problems?

At the crack of dawn,
I awoke startled
and couldn't stop my
tears.

"I hear you, Elon."
My throat choked.
"I understand every bit of your
pain."

Shattered Nerves

After another night of little sleep,
she wakes up to an empty house.

The kids have moved out for good.
That's okay. She still has her friends,
a lot of them.

The coffee boosts her
out of the house
for a daily walk.

Kids weave their bicycles
from one shoulder edge
to the other.

She remembers when
she used to do
that on her Sting-Ray.

Nowadays, it's like walking on eggshells
as she edges against traffic
just alongside the neighborhood front yards.

A car approaches. She slows her pace,
leans toward a mailbox,
and gives the driver a hard stare.

The car passes by.
She breathes out a sigh of relief
and picks up the pace.

But then a car is zooming
toward her from behind.
The back of her ears tingle.

The car zooms by.
The tingle extends to her
arms and throat.

She holds a hand to her heart
and picks up the pace.

The afternoon is even more unnerving.

Drained after loading the car with junk,
she drives to the scrapyard, then pounds
her palm on the steering wheel
upon approaching the shut gate and "closed" sign.

Still, she has time to purchase shoes for tomorrow's
river rafting trip. But the salesclerk tells her they're
sold out of her size. Her stomach wants to shake
like her washing machine.

As she jerks her car onto her driveway,
the sun lowers, and shadows lengthen.
She plops down on the couch,
needing more than ever to soothe her nerves.

But she can't call him anymore because he doesn't drink.
So, she feels so alone
except when she's with her friends, who always offer her
one, and it feels so good.

Precipice

I was admiring the old man's craftwork.
He stood on the other side of the lengthwise-cut
log. In the heavily sloped forest of firs, it hung
like a diving board leading into the abyss.

I told him I was taking pictures
of this mountain bike trial
for a friend of mine's son.

He shook his head and chortled.
"Yeah, well you know nowadays,
kids just can't do any worse
than us adults."

I sighed and laughed along with him.
"Ain't that a fact."

"That's right." He traced his boot
in the rakcd soil alongside the log,
then gazed up at me.

"They just keep looking and looking
at us funny." One side of his face grimaced.
"Kind of an expression that says, 'what?' "

Crepuscular Rays

Nice try buddy,
but you're still stuck
with me,
and it's for the best.

For I'll continue
to take good care of you
just as I've always done
ever since I died.

And you, and only you,
know that for all the shit
I put you through,
you deserve it.

"Yeah, well that's some
journey you just put me
through with that last
woman."

I did it to show you
that you're pure,
and I made you
pure.

For all that I put through,
you remained faithful,
and that's what made you
pure.

"Yeah, well I'm sorry
about our son."

Hey, those things happen.
Just continue
to show him
your unconditional love.

Trust me,
you did it with me.
I'm sure you
can do it with him.

www.ingramcontent.com/pod-product-compliance
Ingram Content Group UK Ltd.
Pitfield, Milton Keynes, MK11 3LW, UK
UKHW041316190726
13845UKWH00025B/307

9 789363 544956